TRACK & FIELD BASICS

by Fred McMane

Illustrated by
Art Seiden

•

Photographs by
Jacob Brown

•

Created and Produced by
Arvid Knudsen

•

PRENTICE-HALL, INC.

Englewood Cliffs, New Jersey

Sports Basics Books

Book design by Arvid Knudsen.

Printed in the United Sates of America.

Prentice-Hall International, Inc., London
Prentice-Hall of Australia, Pty. Ltd., Sydney
Prentice-Hall Canada, Inc., Toronto
Prentice-Hall of India Private Ltd., New Delhi
Prentice-Hall of Japan, Inc., Tokyo
Prentice-Hall of Southeast Asia Pte. Ltd., Singapore
Whitehall Books Limited, Wellington, New Zealand
Editora Prentice-Hall Do Brasil LTDA., Rio de Janeiro

10 9 8 7 6 5 4 3 2 1
Library of Congress Cataloging in Publication Data

McMane, Fred.
 Track and field basics.

 Includes index.
 Summary. Presents a short history of track athletics
and instructions in technique for the various events.
 1. Track-athletics—Juvenile literature.
[1. Track and field]   I. Title.
GV1060.5.M37   1983   796.4′2   82-21458
ISBN 0-13-925966-X

CONTENTS

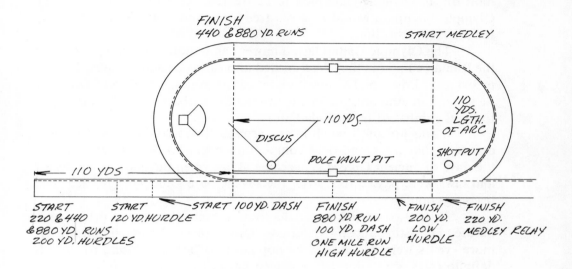

A BRIEF HISTORY 1

Competition in track-and-field events began more than 2,000 years ago in Greece. The ancient Greeks were the world's first great athletes. They ran sprints and tough endurance races and excelled at discus-throwing and shot-putting.

The Greeks originated the first Olympic Games in 776 B.C. The games—festivals that combined patriotism, religion, and athletics—were held every four years. The first track-and-field event is said to have consisted merely of a 200-yard foot-race near the small city of Olympia, but the games gained in scope and became demonstrations of national pride.

In the beginning, the Olympic Games were open only to athletes of pure Greek blood, but later on athletes from other countries were allowed to compete.

5

Although the Greeks were recognized as amateur sportsmen, they were professional in their approach to sports. Greek athletes, like the mythical gods the people worshipped, were revered; and it was not uncommon for an Olympic champion to be treated like a god. Quite often an Olympic champion would be given free room and board in his home city for the rest of his life.

The Olympic Games lasted more than a thousand years, but under the Roman emperors they deteriorated into carnivals and circuses. Finally, in 394 A.D., Emperor Theodosius banned the games. The Romans took little interest in athletics, preferring instead the barbaric life-or-death hand-to-hand combat of trained gladiators.

It was not until much later—around the middle of the eighteenth century—that track-and-field competition began to flourish as it had in the days of ancient Greece. This came about when dueling was abolished and laws were passed to restrict the savage bare-knuckle fights that had become popular.

At first, the track-and-field contests were simple and primitive in nature, consisting mostly of cross-country races. Gradually, however, more events were added. As the popularity of athletes began to spread, definite rules were adopted, and men began to undergo proper training before taking part in a race. By the middle of the nineteenth century, most schools were taking a keen interest in track-and-field competition, and universities began holding championships.

In 1896 the Olympic Games were reborn and held in Athens, Greece. They were the result of efforts by Baron Pierre de Coubertin, a French educator, to promote interest in education and culture, and to foster better international understanding through the universal medium of youth's love of athletics.

Baron de Coubertin enlisted nine nations to send athletes to the first modern Olympics in 1896; now more than 100 nations compete.

Since 1896, the Olympic Games have been held every four years with the exception of 1916, 1940, and 1944, when the world was at war. Several countries, including the United States, did boycott the 1980 Olympics in Moscow in opposition to the Soviet Union's military invasion of Afghanistan. But it is expected that in 1984, all nations will compete again, and track-and-field events will be among the most important.

2 THE TRAINING REQUIRED

The first thing to remember about training for an event is that the same rules don't apply for everyone. No two bodies are exactly the same, so getting into proper shape is also not the same for everyone.

It's not the number of hours you train that's important; it's what you put into it that counts. The *way* in which you approach training is important. If you have no enthusiasm for training, you might as well not do it.

Training concerns the mind as well as the body. Its aim is to build a competent body and a mind that has confidence in that body.

Many youngsters wonder which track-and-field event they should choose. You should choose what you do best.

Are you faster than your friends during short races in gym class? Then maybe you are best suited for the sprints.

Do you have lots of stamina and endurance? Then maybe the long-distance races are for you.

Are you stockily built, with broad and powerful shoulders? Perhaps one of the weight events is more suited to your skills.

There aren't any hard-and-fast rules. But it is best to concentrate on one event and try to master it.

The most important part of your body when it comes to training for a track-and-field event is your lungs. The job of the lungs is to give the heart a steady supply of air. If they don't do this properly, then your heart works less effectively.

In order to become an accomplished runner, you must build up the stamina in your lungs. There is a simple exercise you can do to help get your lungs in shape: put both arms straight out sideways, bring the fingertips back to touch your shoulder, and then push them out again in a fist. This exercise helps to train you in deep steady breathing.

Next do it while jogging for a distance of 50 yards. Jogging makes demands on your lungs, but the arm movements regulate your lungs to the deep and rhythmic breathing that a runner needs.

This exercise you can do almost anywhere. If you increase the distance daily, you will find you puff and pant less.

Concentrate on breathing through your nose, for it means you'll always have a reserve supply to use in sprints and fast finishes.

Once you have learned how to build up the stamina in your lungs, you must learn to run properly. Most people run on heel and toe, but this is incorrect. Learn to run on the balls of your feet. Heel-and-toe running may seem easier and more relaxed at first, but after a while it takes a heavy toll on your strength and puts a strain on your legs that drastically reduces your speed. Once you have mastered the proper way, you will find you can run much faster with far less effort.

Good running technique can also help in the approach for high-jumping, long-jumping, and pole-vaulting.

No matter what event you may be participating in, the same general training program can be followed. For breathing and fitness in general, a lap around the track at a slow jog is a good start, followed by five minutes of limbering-up exercises—the kind you do in gym class.

After loosening up, work at your event, stressing proper form or style rather than speed or distance. Finally, work on bettering your time and/or height and distance.

Many track-and-field athletes today are into weight-training as a method of improving their strength and stamina. Weight-training is an accepted method of training for developing muscles and strength, but it should only be undertaken under competent direction and special planning. The training program should be scientifically designed in order to benefit each individual. Your coach will know best at what age you should begin working with weights and whether such training will be beneficial to your particular event.

Off-season conditioning also is important if you want to be in shape for the season. A daily routine of running some short distances provides light training without inconvenience. Indoor tennis and swimming are also good ways to keep in condition, because they help you use a large number of muscles.

However, there is more to staying in condition than just exercise. Proper diet, rest, and personal hygiene are equally important.

The *regularity* of meals is much more important than what you eat. Drinking plenty of water is also necessary, and so is getting enough sleep. A person who is still growing needs more sleep than an adult.

Keeping warm when not actually running or jumping is essential. Most athletes stay in a track suit or a sweater right up to the last moment before an event begins so their muscles will not stiffen up. If your muscles feel knotted after a strenuous competition, take a hot bath to relax.

Although track-and-field events are basically individual sports, many coaches recommend that a track-and-field squad be divided into equal or nearly equal teams. The fun of competition and individual progress is better achieved by working together.

SPRINTING 3

Running as fast as you can over a short distance may not seem difficult, but it is not as easy as it looks.

In simple terms, a sprinter must attain maximum speed in the shortest amount of time possible in order to compete successfully. To do this he must develop a quick start, be able to accelerate rapidly, and hold his maximum speed over the required distance.

There are three general areas which can be worked on to improve a sprinter's performance: technical, physiological, and psychological. You must cut down on wasted motion in order to get the body moving at a high speed in a short time. Technical areas to improve include the start, stride length, stride cadence, and movement patterns of the body. Proper training can improve your stamina, muscular strength, and flexibility. A sprinter must also have the proper psychological approach. You must know the opponents' strengths and weaknesses as well as your own, and you must train your mind to think "positive" about a race.

Since sprints are usually won by less than a yard—or one tenth of a second—it is extremely important that you get off to a good start. More races are lost at the starting line than anywhere else. The shorter the race, the more important the start becomes.

There are two commands given by the starter before he fires the pistol to start a race. The first is, "On your marks," at which time the sprinter places his feet securely in the starting blocks, one at a time. The feet should be straight and vertical in the blocks, with the weight evenly distributed between the hands and feet. The head should be in natural alignment with the trunk of the body, with the eyes focused slightly in front of the starting line. The arms should be straight, with the hands supported by a high bridge of the fingers and thumb, and placed about a shoulder width apart.

The placement of the blocks is important. Use your own body segments to provide proper measurement of the spacing between the blocks. The front pedal should be approximately 2 to 2½ foot-lengths from the starting line, depending on the distance between the two blocks.

The second command given by the starter is, "Set." Upon hearing that, your eyes, brain, and legs should be on ready alert. The hips should be raised and rear leg straightened, so that the center of gravity has shifted forward. The shoulders also will move slightly ahead of the hands. The angle at the knee of the front leg is approximately 90 degrees. The eyes should be focused somewhere in front of the starting line or down the track. Concentrate on your initial movement actions rather than listening for the sound of the gun.

At the sound of the gun, be ready to "explode" from the blocks. The forward thrust of your right leg aided by rapid arm action and a following thrust from your left leg should bring you into a correct sprinting position after the first few yards. Your stride at this stage will be fairly short, probably not more than about 30 to 35 inches, but this lengthens rapidly. If you're running correctly, you should reach a maximum stride after about 20 yards. Your stride lengths will depend on your height and leg length. Try not to overstride. A stride that is too long for you will slow you down. Work with your coach in determining a stride length, combined with the proper number of strides per second (stride cadence), that is most productive for the overall race.

By the halfway mark of a race, you should be at top speed, and this should continue until about the 80-yard mark of a 100-yard dash. The last 20 yards of a race separate the champions from the also-rans. There may

13

BUNCHED START   MEDIUM START   ELONGATED START

"TAKE YOUR MARK"   "SET"   "GO"

be a temptation at the 80-yard mark to lean back on your heels and straighten your body, but if you do that it will reduce your speed.

When you near the finish line, don't aim for the tape but for an imaginary line about five yards beyond it. Otherwise, your speed will slacken in the last two or three yards and give your rivals a last-second advantage.

Don't stop suddenly as soon as you've passed the tape. Your muscles are being stretched to the limit, and if you pull up suddenly, you're likely to pull a muscle.

Much of the same techniques apply in running the sprints from 50 to 220 yards. However, the 440 (quarter-mile) requires a different approach. It is partly a sprint and partly a distance race. Stamina is more important than speed when racing a 440- or 400-meter event.

There are essentially three parts to a quarter-mile race—a short sprint, a good pace, and another sprint. Success in the quarter-mile race lies in learning to hold a steady, rapid, and effortless stride throughout the middle 300 yards.

14

Psychology plays a tremendous role in the quarter-mile event. Much of the art of winning lies in outwitting the opposition. Knowing your opponents' strengths and weaknesses is important. If you know that he has a tremendous burst of speed but little staying power, then you don't have to worry if he takes an early lead, providing you are able to stay close. Your chance to pass him will come when he begins to take a breather.

If he shows no sign of sprinting ability but has lots of stamina, then your tactics will be different. He will probably stay to the back of the pack at the start and will try to overtake one runner after another during the middle part of the race. If you have confidence in your own sprinting ability, don't waste energy trying to prevent him from overtaking you. Once he's in front, make sure you are near enough to overtake him in the final sprint to the wire.

Patience and determination are essential. Aggressiveness is also a necessary characteristic. The quarter-mile puts great stress on the body. If you haven't yet reached your full height and muscular development, take it easy in all forms of training for the quarter-mile and longer distances so you don't put more strain on your heart and lungs than they can handle.

HITTING THE TAPE

THE HURDLE

HURDLING 4

Many people consider hurdling to be the most beautiful event in track. Runners at full speed gliding over a series of hurdles blend together speed, agility, and courage.

A good hurdler needs tremendous concentration, speed, rhythm, balance, and determination.

You must learn to *run* over the hurdles, not *jump* over them. This means you must run fast, manage your steps so that you're in a position to clear the hurdles, and clear the hurdles smoothly.

There are two types of hurdle races—the 120-yard high hurdles and the 440-yard intermediate hurdles. In the 120-yard event, the hurdles are 42 inches high and are set 10 yards apart. In high school events, the height of the hurdles is shortened to 39 inches. From the start of the race to the first hurdle and from the last hurdle to the finish line there is a distance of 15 yards.

In the 440 event, the hurdles are 36 inches high. The distance from the start to the first hurdle is 49¼ yards, and the 10 hurdles are 38¼ yards apart. The distance from the tenth hurdle to the finish line is 46½ yards.

A youngster considering doing the hurdles should be at least 5 feet 10 inches tall. Anyone shorter than that will have trouble clearing the high hurdles.

17

Since a hurdler makes a lot of unnatural movements with his legs, it is important that he exercise properly to make the legs as supple as possible. Never attempt hurdling without first warming up properly with at least 10 minutes of stretching exercises, as well as jogging. Some good stretching exercises include swinging your leg from the hip while holding onto a bar, trunk-twisting, and trying to touch your chin to your knee while sitting on the ground.

The first thing a hurdler must learn is which leg to lead with. It's better to lead with your left leg.

Determining the number of steps to take between hurdles also is very important. Most hurdlers take eight steps from the starting line to the first hurdle, but taller athletes use only seven. It is important to work out your own stride plan and stick with it. Remember, though, that your takeoff point should be about 6½ to 7½ feet in front of the hurdle.

In clearing the hurdle, a positive approach is important. As you reach the takeoff point, your body should be aimed straight ahead at the middle of the hurdle. When you begin your takeoff, the knee of the takeoff leg should be lifted up high and hard, and the opposite arm should move straight out forward from the shoulder and be parallel with the lead leg. The head and chest should be lowered, with the body thrust forward from the waist. If all these actions are done positively and forcefully, you should have no trouble in clearing the hurdle quickly.

Once you've cleared the hurdle, you will find you're right into the next step and on your way toward the second hurdle.

It is good to practice clearing one hurdle before you take on another, but as you master each one, keep adding another one. It may be a good idea to start with the hurdle at its lowest point, until you get the rhythm you need. Then, after you've mastered three low hurdles, gradually keep raising the height to 42 inches.

In practicing for the hurdles, sprinting should be part of your daily program. Also include several hurdle practice runs and exercises to increase stamina.

If you're concentrating on the intermediate hurdles, then a lot of middle-distance training is necessary. Stride control, pace judgment, and endurance are more important than speed and hurdling-ability in the intermediate event.

Although the intermediate hurdles are six inches lower, your energy must be distributed more carefully. A quarter-mile hurdler must also be a good quarter-miler.

The left-leg lead is very important in intermediate hurdling, since much of the race is contested around a curve. The left leg helps the hurdler keep better balance when he lands. A right-footed hurdler is thrown to the outside of the lane, forcing him to run three extra yards.

RELAY-RACING— TEAMWORK-RUNNING 5

Relay-racing is a team-oriented event in a sport that is geared toward individual achievement. It is one of the most exciting events of a track meet and serves as a good way of judging the overall strength of a team. It also gives coaches an opportunity to get their second-class sprinters into the act.

Relay teams consist of four sprinters, each of whom runs approximately the same distance. For example, in a 400-meter relay, each sprinter would run 100 meters; in a 1,600-meter relay, each would race 400 meters.

The key to good relay-racing is the baton pass. The baton, a hollow cylinder about a foot in length, is passed from hand to hand at the end of each "leg" of the race. It must be exchanged within 20 yards of a change-over zone and must be retained throughout the race. If a changeover is fumbled and the baton drops to the ground, the runner who dropped it will be disqualified, and his team will finish last.

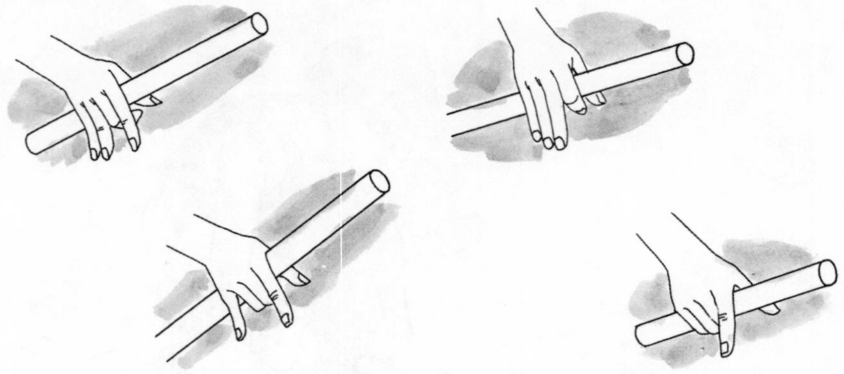

The shorter the relay, the more important the baton pass becomes. The baton should be kept moving at top speed throughout the relay. With proper and well-timed passing, it is possible to defeat a team of better runners whose exchanges are inferior.

Proper timing is essential in passing the baton. Both runners should be at maximum speed in the short relays when the exchange is made. It takes much practice to become efficient at passing the baton.

The recommended technique of passing the baton is the "flip-flop" method. The first runner carries the baton in the right hand and passes it to the second runner's left hand. The second runner passes it to the third runner's right hand, and the third runner passes it to the anchor leg's left hand.

For a smooth, efficient baton pass, the outgoing runner should mark off a spot where he wants the exchange to be made, then time his approach so that he is going at full speed when he reaches the exchange point. When the outgoing runner reaches the exchange point, he should put the hand back, palm up, and give a steady target to the incoming runner. Ideally, the exchange should be made with both runners' arms fully extended.

BATON EXCHANGES

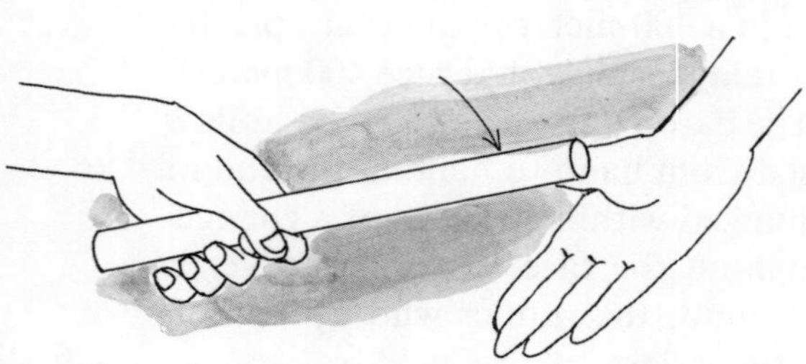

VISUAL PASS
THE PASSER'S AND
RECEIVER'S HAND
POSITIONS

NON-VISUAL PASS
THE PASSER'S AND
RECEIVER'S HAND
POSITIONS

CHECK POINT

RESTRAINING LINE
11 YDS.

RUNNING AT TOP SPEED
PASSING ZONE 22 YDS.

PASSING BATON
15-18 YDS.

It takes split-second timing. If the outgoing runner leaves his mark too soon, he will either run away from the baton or have to slow down. If the outgoing runner starts too late, the runners will be too close together and the distance lost can never be regained.

Staying within the changeover zone when the exchange of the baton takes place is vital. In the 1960 Rome Olympics, the United States' 400-meter relay team was disqualified because a runner ran out of his passing zone on the second leg. It is the responsibility of the incoming runner to make a good pass to the outgoing runner, so the latter can focus his full attention on a fast start.

In longer distance relays, baton-passing is not quite as critical, and the responsibility for a good exchange rests with the outgoing runner, due to the fatigue of the incoming runner. In these relays, the outgoing runner should turn around and look at the incoming runner to receive the baton. The pass should be made from the incoming runner's right hand to the outgoing runner's left hand, and the outgoing runner should time his takeoff based on how strongly the incoming runner is finishing the last 200 meters.

Choosing a running order is important, and much thought should be given to the personality and temperament of each runner. Generally, the fastest runner runs the anchor leg, and the second fastest the first leg. The second and third runners must be very reliable in both receiving and passing the baton, since they must execute both. The anchor runner must be someone who performs well under pressure.

It is important to remember that the team with the four fastest runners does not guarantee the fastest relay team. Speed and teamwork combined are the keys to a successful relay team.

CURVE RUNNING

DISTANCE-RUNNING AND ENDURANCE EVENTS 6

Distance-running is one of the greatest tests of physical and mental endurance. It requires strength, stamina, and tremendous concentration. In addition, tactics are extremely important. Knowing how to pace yourself and when to make your move are the keys to running a successful distance race.

If you have discovered that you are not fast enough to compete in the sprints or the 440, then you might consider the middle distances. The half-mile, or 880-run, offers a good test of your stamina. But, if you don't believe your legs and lungs are ready for the 880, then don't try it.

In running an 880, keeping an even pace is very important. It is the first transition from a sprint to a run, and an even pace must be kept in all four segments of the race.

A middle-distance runner must learn to relax and keep his balance, using a smooth, controlled leg movement, hip rotation, and arm action. A basic rule to remember is the slower the race, the shorter the stride; the faster the race, the longer the stride.

STRIDES AND BODY MOTIONS FOR DISTANCE RUNNING

A mile must be thought of as four different segments, with a different pace for each. The first lap is run briskly, the second is taken fairly easily with a comfortable stride, the third lap is a slow one in which you concentrate on saving energy, and the fourth begins slowly but often ends with a rapid burst of speed.

The third quarter is the crucial phase of all tactical mile-running. There is usually a tendency during the third quarter of the race for the runner to grow tired, both mentally and physically. A good miler must learn to overcome this fatigue without straining or losing the rhythm of stride.

The main work in overtaking the runners ahead of you in any distance race should come in the last 220 yards. Success depends on how well you've been able to judge positions and the condition of those in front. A smart runner does not make a sudden sprint to the finish line, but does a series of sudden bursts that catch his opponent unaware.

Training techniques for distance-running vary, but all coaches agree that speed work is essential. Uphill-running at various grades and distances is a good way to develop speed and strength; and downhill-running is excellent for building up leg speed. Better distance-running is based on more running—and the *intensity* of training is fundamental. Strength-training—such as pull-ups, sit-ups, and light weight-lifting—also is recommended on a daily basis.

During the off-season, cross-country running is recommended for building up legs and lungs. For a miler with good speed, cross-country running is considered sound stamina work for a three- or four-month off-season period. For runners lacking good speed, the cross-country routine should be mixed with one or two days of speed work each week.

Long-distance running requires different training techniques and skills. To begin with, the length of your stride must be cut down to avoid exhaustion. Also, since speed is much less important than endurance, your body should be more erect and arm and leg movements should be much shorter than in middle-distance running.

You must learn to run at a completely steady pace, and this can come only by lapping the track over and over again while keeping track of your time. Break the race up into short segments and run them repeatedly to develop speed and pace judgment and to build endurance.

In long-distance running, the training of the mind is as important as the training of the body. You have to overcome the mental tiredness that can often prove your undoing long before your body gives out.

Long-distance running can also be very monotonous, so you must think of something to occupy your mind. Some runners recite poetry, others think about their hobbies. It is important that your mind does not think about the tremendous strain that your body is undergoing.

ARMS ARE SWUNG FORWARD FOR BALANCE

7 LONG-JUMPING

Jumping for distance requires exceptional running speed and tremendous muscular power.

There are two types of distance-jumping—the long jump (or broad jump) and the triple jump, more commonly referred to as the hop, step, and jump. In both forms of jumping, speed is essential to a good takeoff.

Sprinters have always made the best performers at this event. Jesse Owens and Carl Lewis, two of the greatest long-jumpers of all time, also were standout sprinters.

The object of the long jump is to take a running start, hit the takeoff board (set in the ground) without stepping beyond it, and leap as far as possible into a landing pit filled with sand. Your distance will be measured from the pit side of the takeoff board to the nearest mark in the sand made by any part of your body.

It is important to know which is your takeoff foot. Most right-handed people will push off with the left foot. A simple way to find out is to run a few steps and bound into the air. After a few times notice which foot you tend to push off with.

After you've determined which foot is your takeoff foot, find out where the best spot is to begin your jump. Determine where to begin your run so that you arrive at the takeoff on the proper foot well prepared to jump.

A jumper should attain the maximum speed that he can control in order to get a well-balanced takeoff. Often a jumper will be going at about 95 percent of his top speed before beginning his jump. Running speed should peak about four strides from the takeoff board, so proper stride is essential.

Concentrate on the takeoff. When you reach your takeoff spot, drive smoothly off the board and concentrate on keeping your takeoff foot directly under your hip. If you cross your takeoff foot over to the other side of your body, it will make you lose your balance and will result in a poor jump.

As you begin your takeoff, shift your line of sight from the board to the horizon. Concentrate on keeping your chest up and getting your knees up. Ideally, you should go up and come down at a 45-degree angle.

There are two styles of flight—the hang and the hitch-kick. Both help you land smoothly.

In using the hang technique, as you take off bring your trail leg alongside your lead leg with your knees apart and slightly bent. Raise your arms over your head, so it appears that you are hanging from a crossbar. Now as you get ready to land, bring your arms forward, which will raise your legs and bring them forward as well.

The hitch-kick method takes great coordination and resembles a person running in air. At the takeoff, your lead knee comes to hip height, followed by your takeoff leg, followed again by the lead leg. Now both legs are in an extended position in front.

When you land, carry your momentum forward; don't fall backward and leave marks in the sand behind your feet. Your arms should

LONG-JUMP

a) TAKE-OFF   b) KNEE-TUCK   c) LANDING   d) ARMS BALANCE FORWARD

29

reach forward over your feet, and your legs should be extended almost horizontally forward. You should break the sand with your heels, and your head and shoulders should be hunched forward of your knees to help you carry your momentum forward. A jumper should end on his hands and knees.

A long-jumper should always exercise to strengthen the knees and thighs, since they absorb so much impact on takeoff. Sprinting and low-hurdling are also good conditioners. Sprinting helps to build up speed, and low-hurdling helps to improve stride control.

In the triple jump, the first movement must be a "hop." That means the jumper must land and take off from the same foot used at the takeoff board. The second movement is a strike, or "skip," onto the other foot, from which the final jump is made. If the ground is touched at any point between these three stages, the jump will not count. Each stage in the triple jump is important and must be worked on separately.

In the hop, your body weight should be clearly over the takeoff foot to permit a balanced flight, landing on the same foot. The knee of your takeoff foot should be flexed so that the "step" phase will be natural.

After landing on the "hop," the left leg passes the right leg and is pulled up, bent at the knee. The body leans forward, and both arms are drawn back to assist in gaining height at takeoff for the final jump.

In the "jump" portion, height is the goal, just as in the long jump. The flight and landing are the same as in the long jump, with an emphasis on maintaining good balance and keeping your feet up until the last moment.

Since the legs take tremendous strain in jumping, don't make too many jumps in practice. The risk of injury is great. A varied training program of exercises to strengthen the legs, with low hurdles, sprint-racing, and jumping is recommended.

FOSBURY FLOP

STRADDLE

JUMPING FOR HEIGHT 8

High Jump

To be a good high-jumper, you need strong stomach and leg muscles. And you must develop and perfect your style of jumping.

Style is very important. There are three basic styles—the scissors, the straddle, and the flop. The flop, developed by Dick Fosbury, who won the 1968 Olympic gold medal, is the most common style in the United States among experienced high-jumpers. But the straddle is the more accepted style among European jumpers.

Both of these styles are difficult to learn, so it might be best to start off by learning the scissors. Once you have mastered the art of getting over the bar, then you can learn the flop or the straddle method.

In learning to high-jump, start the bar at a low height. This allows you to perfect your style. In the scissors method of jumping, approach the bar slightly from the right, using your left foot for takeoff. As you approach the takeoff, drop both arms back and forcefully lift them to shoulder height as you plant your takeoff foot. Your right leg comes up and drops over the bar, and the left leg follows in scissorlike fashion. You will land on your right foot first, followed by your left.

In order to achieve competitive heights, you must learn either the flop or the straddle. Both require great concentration and hours of practice to perfect.

With the flop, you need a foam-rubber landing pit. Without one you risk injury, since you will be landing on your shoulders. If a foam-rubber pit is not available, don't attempt to learn the flop.

In the flop, approach the bar in sort of a modified curve, or *J* pattern, and jump over the bar backward. The approach run is generally 9 to 11 steps, and after the fifth step, begin curving in toward the bar. Running through a quarter circle allows you to build up the force necessary to carry you over the bar after takeoff.

In the final steps to the takeoff, accelerate slightly by shortening your stride length. This is done to lower the center of gravity upon takeoff.

In the takeoff, bring your right knee and both arms up strongly to the height of your shoulders. Arch your back and bring your arms down close to your sides as the bar is cleared. As your torso clears the bar, lift your knees and feet to clear the bar.

If you hit the bar on the way up, you're taking off too close to the bar. If you're hitting the bar on the way down, you're taking off too far from the bar.

The straddle is much different from the flop. The approach is made in a straight line, and different parts of the body clear the bar one after another.

Speed is essential in the straddle to generate the power necessary to clear the bar. An eight-step run is used most often, and the takeoff should be made with a strong upward thrust of both arms and the lead knee. The body is driven upward and the right arm and right side clear the bar first. Getting the trail leg over is the difficult part. Raise your lead arm up and turn the shoulders in the opposite direction to the direction the trail leg is moving. The trail leg should then lift over the bar.

In training for the high jump, it is necessary to develop strength, suppleness, and style. Working with weights to improve muscle tone is recommended. Light jogging also is good to keep limbs supple enough for jumping. High kicking and touching the toes without bending the knees are good exercises for keeping the muscles loose.

A high-jumper should also work daily on improving his speed. Sprints of 20 to 30 yards are a good exercise, and running over hurdles gets the stride pattern correct.

It is important to keep your body warm when not jumping so that your muscles remain relaxed and supple.

POLE-VAULTING

THE APPROACH

THE PLANT

THE TAKE-OFF

STRING
AND
ROCK BACK

PULL TURN RELEASE

Pole Vault

Pole-vaulters are like gymnasts in that it takes tremendous agility, upper body strength, balance, and courage to be good.

Pole-vaulting is the most complex of all track-and-field events. Success depends greatly on the proper planting of the pole into the box. Originally, vaulters used bamboo poles. Later, aluminum was used. However, the fiberglass pole is used exclusively now, and its flexibility allows for greater heights to be attained.

In selecting a pole, look for one that can hold 5 to 10 pounds more than your body weight. The pole should be held with the right hand up the pole, palm up, and the left hand lower, palm down. Control is important, so you should use a grip which is secure but not too tight. A wide hand spread of about 12 to 18 inches will allow the pole to bend properly.

In carrying the pole, hold it close to the body and almost parallel to the ground, with the front end slightly downward. Shoulders should be relaxed and squared, the front arm flexed, and the back arm slightly bent.

Speed in the approach run is important in achieving great heights. However, it isn't how fast you run that counts, but how well you control that speed so that the approach is smooth.

As mentioned before, the most significant step in pole-vaulting is the planting of the pole in the box before the takeoff. With a fiberglass pole, the pole should be placed into the box at the last stride so that the takeoff foot and pole hit at the same time. The pole should be held above the head when you slide it into the box.

On the takeoff, your right knee should be bent, while your chest and hips drive forward into the pole. Concentrate on keeping the pole in front of your chest, and let the pole do most of the work. Your momentum plus the action of the pole should carry you up. Your right leg will straighten as your left leg catches up to it. As your hips rise to the level of your head, draw your knees up into the pole. Try to get your hips as high as possible and behind the pole.

When the pole is almost straight, begin to pull and turn your body over the crossbar. The pull and turn should be a very quick and powerful movement as you finally extend your arms straight down the pole. As the arms are extended downward, your left arm reaches its full extension first, then the right arm is released. In effect, you are doing a handstand on the pole. Your arms are then lifted quickly away from the crossbar. The pole is pushed one way and you go the other way and land in the pit.

Gymnastic exercises and weight-lifting are necessary training for pole-vaulters. Long-distance running, at least once a week, also can help your endurance.

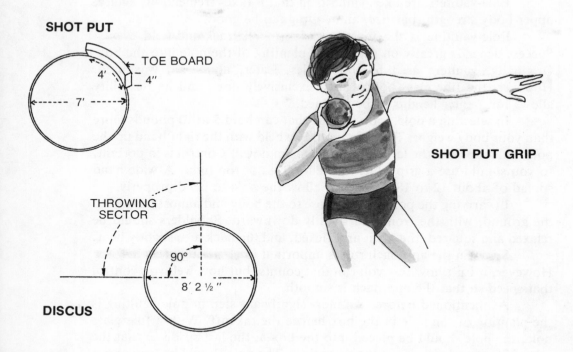

SHOT PUT

TOE BOARD

4'

4"

7'

SHOT PUT GRIP

THROWING SECTOR

90°

8' 2 ½"

DISCUS

⑨ THE GREAT THROWING EVENTS

Most athletes who participate in the throwing events—such as the shot put, javelin, discus, and hammer—are big and strong. But size and strength alone are not enough to perform well in these events. Agility and timing are as important.

In all throwing events, the speed at which the implement is released plays a large part in how far it will go. It has been proven that a 10 percent increase in speed of release in shot-putting and discus-throwing produces an increase of as much as 21 percent in distance.

Not only is it important for an athlete to learn the most advantageous throwing technique and to follow the most beneficial training program, it is also important for him to select the throwing implement that will provide the greatest possible distance.

Shot Put

A shot put is a solid ball of iron, steel, or brass, weighing from 12 to 16 pounds for boys and men and from 8 pounds to 8 pounds 13 ounces for girls and women. In high school, boys compete with a 12-pound shot and girls with an eight-pound shot. In college and international competitions, the shot weighs 16 pounds for men and 8 pounds 13 ounces for women.

There is a slight advantage in selecting a shot that is smaller in size. U.S. high school rules allow the 12-pound shot to be as small as 3⅞ inches in diameter, ¾ of an inch smaller than the maximum size allowed. International rules allow the 16-pound shot to be as small as 4⅜ inches in diameter, also ¾ of an inch smaller than the maximum size allowed.

A smaller shot will travel slightly farther than the larger shot, because it encounters less air resistance in flight.

A shot put is not *thrown*. It is put in a sort of punching motion. The elbow should remain behind the shot at all times. The fist leads and the elbow follows.

The shot is put from a ring which measures 7 feet in diameter. The ring includes a toeboard at the front which measures 4 feet long and 4¼ inches high. The ring is divided in half, and if you step out of the front half or touch the top of the toeboard, you'll receive a foul.

In putting the shot, speed around the ring is important. The shot should travel at a 40- or 45-degree angle from the moment you release it.

The shot should be held deep in the hand on the pads at the base of your fingers, with the thumb and little finger providing support. The wrist should be flexed, and the hand then tucked over the collarbone with the ball touching the neck or jaw. Apply pressure against the neck to hold the shot in.

37

Once you have gotten the proper grip on the shot, learn the proper technique for releasing it. Begin from the back of the ring. The right foot supports the body weight and is placed close to the rear border of the circle, with the left foot placed behind it. The shoulders should be hunched and the back rounded, with the knees bent at approximately 120-degree angles. Your lead arm should be hanging down or reaching across your right to help maintain balance.

When you begin your put, start to turn on your right foot and push off with your right leg. Your left arm leads your body around. As your weight shifts and you begin to straighten out on your left leg, your left arm pulls in sharply and your right arm punches the shot out.

Timing is important. The coach of a shot-putter must watch the athlete at the starting position. Anything that causes imbalance will result in a poor put.

In practicing the shot put, perfect your movement, or glide, in the ring. Practice repeatedly and take several standing puts to practice arm delivery.

Weight-lifting is essential in training to build up strength, but jogging also is recommended to increase endurance.

Discus

The discus throw was one of the events used by the ancient Greeks. The discus itself is a plate-shaped wooden circle framed by a wooden rim. It is 8½ inches in diameter and weighs 3 pounds 9 ounces for high school boys and is 8⅝ to 8¾ inches in diameter and weighs 4 pounds 6.547 ounces for college men. It is 7⅛ to 7¼ inches in diameter and weighs 2 pounds 3½ ounces for women. It is thrown from a circle 8 feet 2½ inches in diameter.

There are two basic grips for holding a discus—one in which all the fingers are spread and another in which the index finger and the middle finger are together. In holding the discus, the tips of the fingers should overlap the edge and the wrist should be firm. The discus should be held so that the index finger is the last to lose contact with the object.

Discus-throwers must have the same qualities as shot-putters. The best discus-throwers are all big, but in addition to strength, agility, coordination, balance, and timing are necessary.

To throw the discus, begin by facing the rear of the circle with your back to the direction of the throwing. Start by taking a few preliminary swings using the entire body. These movements set the rhythm for the throw and prepare the body for movement across the circle.

At the end of the last preliminary swing, start to spin on the ball of your left foot. After turning 180 degrees in a counterclockwise direction, the right foot is raised with the leg rotated from the hip, bringing the right foot down to the ground. As rotation continues, the left foot is pushed out toward the direction of throwing. Upon releasing the discus, the front foot should be in contact with the ground.

The discus will go in the direction your left foot is pointed. The main sources of power throughout the delivery are the legs, hips, and entire body, *not* the throwing arm. To reduce air resistance, the discus should be released at an angle of no more than 30 degrees.

Like shot-putters, discus-throwers should concentrate their training on developing their size and strength and perfecting their technique.

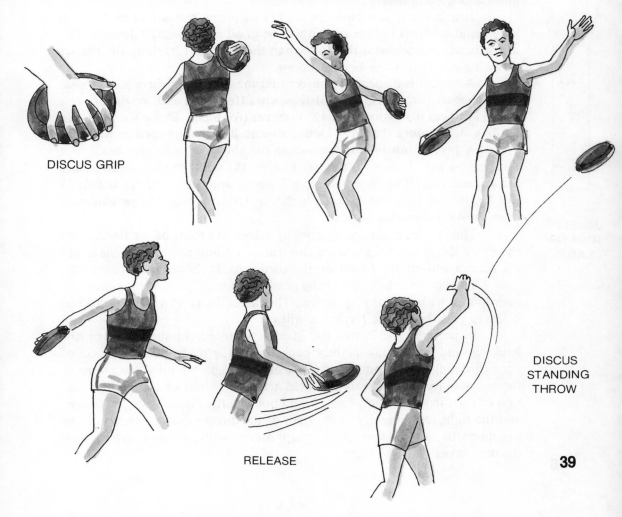

DISCUS GRIP

DISCUS STANDING THROW

RELEASE

a) CARRY OVER SHOULDER   b) FINAL STEP BEFORE THROW   c) READYING FOR THROW   d) THE FOLLOW-THROUGH

Javelin

Javelin-throwers are generally big and strong, but strength is not as vital as it is to discus-throwers and shot-putters. Speed, agility, and quickness are important.

Just because you have the ability to throw a baseball or football long distances does not mean you will be good at throwing a javelin. The throw is made more with the body than the arm, and learning the proper throwing position is the key to success.

A javelin is a spearlike object that measures anywhere from 7 feet 2½ inches (for women) to 8 to 10¼ inches (for men) and weighs not less than 11 ounces (for women) or 12¼ ounces (for men). There is a whipcord binding of no more than 6¼ inches around it, which is used as the grip.

A javelin must be thrown over the shoulder with one hand, not slung or hurled. A throw is not valid unless the point of the javelin strikes the ground first. The throw is made from an approach runway that is 13 feet 1½ inches wide and 98 feet 6 inches to 120 feet long. The javelin must land within a throwing sector.

JAVELIN RUN-UP LANE

The javelin is carried diagonally across the palm of the hand, with the index finger pointing toward the rear or curling around the shaft and the thumb and middle finger on the cord grip. It should be held loosely.

The javelin is held above the head and moved gently as the shoulder coordinates with the running action. The faster the javelin is moving when it leaves your hand, the farther it will go.

In preparing to throw the javelin, your weight should be on the back leg and your body slightly back to get the maximum extension of your throwing arm. Your throwing arm should be extended backward as far as possible, and the lead arm held across the chest or out in the direction of the throw. The left foot should point in the direction of the throw, and the right foot, slightly to the right of the direction of the throw. Most beginners use a six- to eight-step approach, while a more experienced thrower takes 10 to 14 steps.

As you begin your throw, shift your weight from the back leg to the front leg. The javelin is pulled through over your shoulder close to your ear and is released with a snap of the wrist. As you complete your release, your body should fall forward, with your left leg acting as a brake. To get the maximum distance from your throw and to reduce the amount of air resistance, the javelin should be released at an angle of 30 degrees.

Exercises should include building up the back and shoulder muscles. Practicing the throw from a standing position is good to perfect the technique.

Hammer Throw

High schools in only two states in the nation include the hammer throw in their track-and-field event. It is an important event included in college programs and Olympic and pre-Olympic contests. We include it here to provide you with the essential requirements of this unique sporting activity.

Hammer-throwers are generally the biggest in the weight events. The world's greatest at this event, Harold Connolly, was six feet tall and weighed 238 pounds.

The hammer throw is very difficult to learn. Strength contributes a great deal to performance, but a beginner shouldn't be concerned too much with strength. It is technique that is most important. The speed at which the hammerhead is moving before delivery is the key to success in this complex event, and speed can only be achieved if the head travels the correct path.

The hammer itself is a solid steel ball connected to a single length of wire that is looped at the end. The ball and wire together cannot weigh less than 16 pounds and can't be more than four feet long. The wire handle cannot be less than ⅛ inch in diameter and is connected to the ball by a swivel.

The hammer is thrown from a 7-foot circle outlined by a band of wood or metal. It must land in a 60-degree sector. After throwing the hammer, the athlete must leave the circle from the rear half after the hammer has landed. The distance is measured from the nearest point of indentation made by the hammer to the inner edge of the circle.

Hammer-throwers must train regularly for strength with weights and exercises. But technique-training is most important. Train with other hammer-throwers so you'll help each other in establishing proper technique and eliminating bad habits.

10 SCORING—HOW IT IS DONE

A large number of officials are needed to run a successful track meet. The most important official is the referee. His duties are to see that the rules are observed, decide any technical points that arise in a race, decide the winner of an event if the judges are unable to arrive at a unanimous decision, and to assign the duties of the judges. A referee must know track-and-field rules and must be a capable decision-maker.

Judges decide the order in which the competitors finished and also measure and record the heights and distances in all the jumping and weight events.

The timekeeper records the finishing times of the contestants. There are three official timekeepers for each event, one of whom is designated as the chief timekeeper. In major meets, there are also two alternate timekeepers assigned to each race, but their watches are not consulted unless one or more of the official timekeepers' watches fail.

All three of the timekeepers record the time of each running event on their stopwatches. If two of the three watches agree, the time shown by two is the official time. If all three watches disagree, the time shown by the watch recording the middle time is the official time. If only two watches record time and fail to agree, the longer time of the two is accepted as official time. Time is taken from the flash of the pistol to the moment at which any part of the body of the competitor reaches the nearest edge of the finish line.

There are basically two ways in which a track meet is scored. In smaller meets, points are distributed in each event on the basis of 5 points for a first-place finish, 3 for second, 2 for third, and 1 for fourth. In larger meets, points are awarded on the basis of 10 for first, 8 for second, 6 for third, 4 for fourth, 2 for fifth, and 1 for sixth.

The team with the greatest number of points is declared the winner. If teams are tied in point total, the team with the greatest number of first-place finishers is declared the champion.

In cross-country competition, the scoring is different. The winner is determined by the *least* number of points. Points are awarded by order of finish in the race. For example, the winner would be given 1 point, second-place finisher 2 points, and so on. In case of a tie, the team whose member finished nearest to first place is declared the winner.

In the throwing events, each competitor is allowed three trial throws, and the six best after that are allowed three more. Each competitor's best throw is the one that is counted. In all the throwing events, the measurement is made from the nearest mark left by the object after it hits the ground. Also, the competitor cannot leave the throwing area until after the object hits the ground.

In the jumping events, the best of each competitor's jumps is the one that is counted. In the high jump, a competitor is allowed three misses at each height before being eliminated. A jumper is allowed to pass on any height, but in case of a tie, the winner is the one with the best record at the last height cleared.

In the long jump, each competitor gets three jumps, and the six best finishers are allowed three more jumps. Each competitor's best jump is the one which is counted.

Sometimes the number of competitors in the sprints or the hurdles is too large, so it is necessary to hold preliminary rounds. In those instances, those who finish first and second in each qualify for the second round. The winner of the event is the one with the best time in the second round. In races run in lanes, runners must stay in the lane assigned. A runner who runs out of the lane will be disqualified.

11 PREPARING FOR THE BIG EVENT

It is physically and psychologically impossible for athletes to be mentally ready for every competition on the schedule. Most high schools schedule between 12 and 15 meets during the competitive months. The coach should prepare his athletes for the ones that really count.

This is most easily done by placing each meet on the schedule into a specific category. One way is to label each meet as either developmental, important, or crucial. In a *developmental* meet, an athlete would try only to develop his skills. He would work on his technique, or test a different strategy against competition. An *important* meet would be one against a traditional rival, where the athlete would try to do his best against good competition. A *crucial* meet would be against stiff competition in state meets. By classifying meets, each meet is put into perspective, and the coach and the athletes prepare for the ones that really count.

Athletes on the high school level should compete only once a week. A study conducted by the Olympic Development Committee revealed that competing more than once a week does not allow for proper recovery between meets, nor does it allow for proper time for training, and can be detrimental to the athlete's long-term development.

An athlete begins training several months before actual competition begins, but in the week leading up to the scheduled meet, the training schedule should be changed so that the athlete does not peak too early. More difficult workouts should be done earlier in the week. However, it is important not to neglect conditioning programs. Neglecting weight-training during the week, for example, could result in strength loss and be harmful to the final performance.

The mind plays a very important part in an athlete's overall performance. In the days before the competition, the athlete must convince himself that certain goals are attainable. The ability to think positively is essential to quality performance.

Part of the mental preparation for a competition involves the planning of strategy. This is especially important to long-distance runners, but high-jumpers and pole-vaulters also use psychological ploys to increase their chances of winning.

An athlete should keep a daily log of his progress to evaluate training and competition and to help in planning training for the following year. It is important to evaluate each year with the coach and begin preparing for the next year.

At the end of a competitive season, the athlete should concentrate on rest, recovery, and relaxation. Hard physical conditioning for the next season should not begin again for at least six weeks after the previous season is over.

It is important to remember that it is not always the best athlete who wins, but the one who was best prepared at that particular moment.

Afterword

In many ways track and field is the purest of all forms of athletic competition. In primitive times, man's struggle for survival often depended on his ability to run and throw better than his enemies. Through evolution a sport was born that presents a continuing inner struggle and constantly tests man's survival instincts.

It is a sport that offers constant challenge. The challenge is not necessarily geared to winning an event but in competing against oneself.

"There's a lot of emphasis placed on winning and not enough on competing and enjoying it," says Wyomia Tyus, a former Olympic sprint champion.

Track and field also helps build character. Confidence, courage, and determination—all of which go into making up one's character— are natural by-products of track-and-field competition.

Sportsmanship is also learned through competition in track and field. Competing head-to-head with other athletes who have endured the same rigorous training creates respect for one's opponent and appreciation for his accomplishments.

Above all, track and field teaches discipline. It takes single- minded dedication of both the mind and body to compete successfully in the sport. And, of course, self-discipline is the foundation on which is built personal achievement in all walks of life.

Index